INDABA YENOMBOLO

THE NUMBER STORY

SMALL BOOK ONE

ENGLISH - isiNDEBELE

*Numbers Teach Children
Their Number Names*

written and illustrated by

MISS ANNA

Early Reader Edition of *The Number Story 1*
Bronze Medal Winner, 2016 Wishing Shelf Book Award

Library of Congress Control Number: 2018902040

Names: Miss Anna, author.
Title: Number story : numbers teach children their number names / Miss Anna.
Description: Portland, OR: Lumpy Publishing, 2018.
Identifiers: ISBN 978-1-945977-85-5| LCCN 2018902040
Summary: The pictures and rhymes present stories which introduce numbers 0-10.
Subjects: LCSH Numeration—English--Ndebele--Pictorial works--Juvenile literature. | BISAC JUVENILE NONFICTION /
Languages: English--Ndebele
Classification: LCC QA141.3 .M57 2018 | DDC 513—dc23

Publisher: Lumpy Publishing
Website: www.missannabooks.com
Email: missanna@missannabooks.com

Paperback: ISBN 978-1-945977-85-5
Printed in the U.S.A.   1 3 5 7 9 10 8 6 4 2

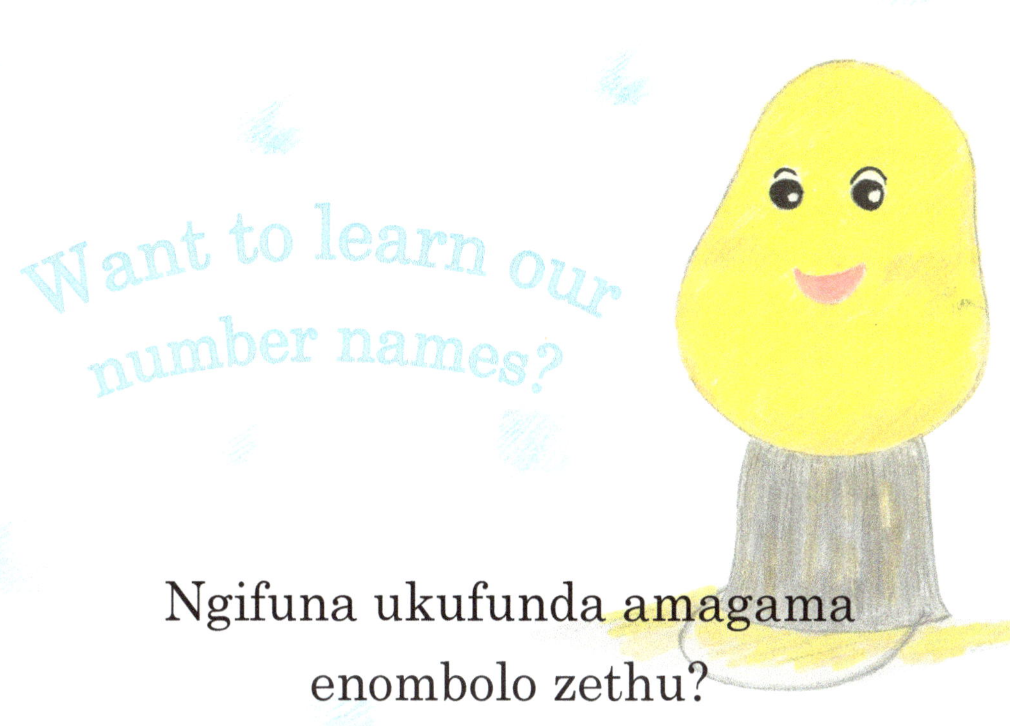

Ngifuna ukufunda amagama
enombolo zethu?

It is very easy and a lot of fun!

Kulula kakhulu njalo kugcwele ngemidlalo!

Say-along our little jingle

Khuluma ugudlisa kuzinanakazana zethu!

starting from Number One!

Sizaqala ngenombolo yethu yakuqala!

1

ONE looks like my one finger.

KUNYE

kuqonde njengomunwe wami.

ONE!
KUNYE!

2

TWO   trails a tail.

KUBILI

kulandelwa ngumsila.

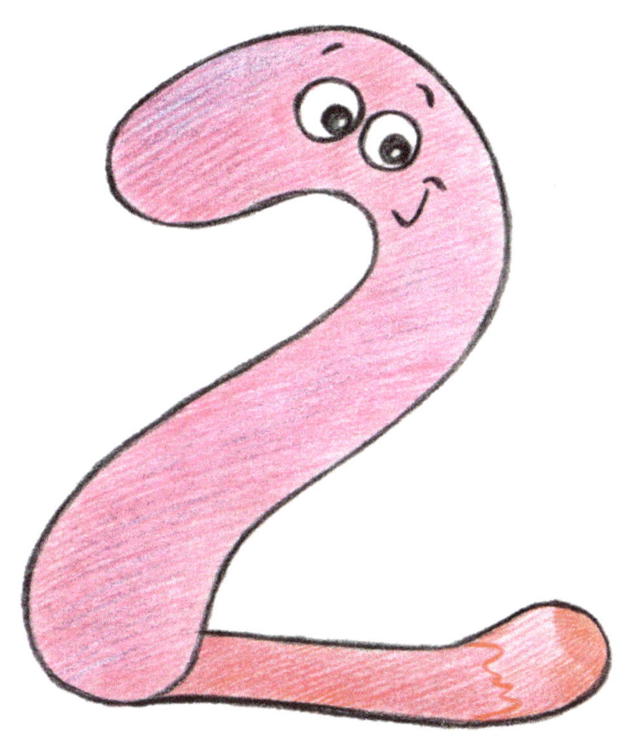

A TAIL! UMSILA!

3

THREE   has bumps.

KUTHATHU
kunjenge amagquma.

BUMPY! AMAGQUMA!

4

FOUR carries a sail.

KUNE

kungumkhumbi.

UMKHUMBI!
Isikebhe esinomkhumbi!

5

FIVE   is a racing track.

KUHLANU

ungowomcintiswano umzila.

VROOM
VROOOM!

6

SIX curves like a snail.

SITHANDATHU ijika umnenke.

A SNAIL! UMNENKE!

7

SEVEN has a sharp angle.

LIKHOMBA

ine-angi ebukhali.

BE CAREFUL! IT'S SHARP!
NANZELELA! KUBUKHALI!

8

EIGHT is rollercoaster rails.

BUNANE

kungumzila we-*rollercoaster*.

YAY!
YIPPEE!

NINE   is a bubble on a stick.

LITHOBA

kuba *bubble* ngenduku.

A BUBBLE! I-BUBBLE!

10

TEN   is an eye of a whale.

ITJHUMI

kulilihlo elodwa enhlanzini.

HELLO!
SAWUBONA!

And
Futhi

0

ZERO   is an empty pail.

ZERO

kuyinkinga engenalutho.

IT'S
EMPTY!

AKULALUTHO!

Thank you for playing with us today.

We had a lot of fun too!

Siyabonga ukudlala lathi lamuhla.

Sibelemidlalo eminengi futhi lathi sikholisil

We are your Number friends,
Zero to Ten,
Who will be here for you~
Singabangane bakho
Zero kuya Kweshumi.
Sizakuba lawe kuze kube laphakade!

Bye-bye now!
See you again soon!
Salakuhle khathesi!
Ngizakubon njalo emalangeni!

The Numbers are *SINGING* too!

To sing-a-long, look for Miss Anna Number Story
at your favorite music store like iTUNES.

MP3

Numbers 0-10
IDENTIFYING
& COUNTING

Numbers 11-20
& Ordinals
first, second, third...

Numbers 0-100
& Place Values
ones, tens, hundreds...

About Clocks
& Telling Time
hours, minutes, seconds

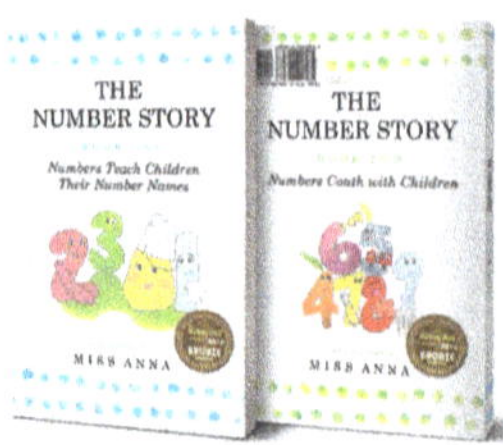

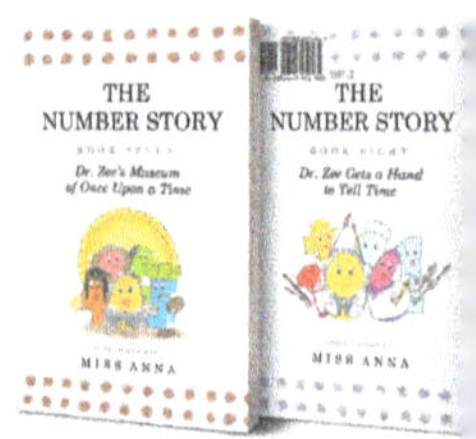

Number Story 1 & 2
isbn: 978-0-996216-48-7

Number Story 3 & 4
isbn: 978-1-945977-01-5

Number Story 5 & 6
isbn: 978-1-945977-06-0

Number Story 7 & 8
isbn: 978-1-949320-40-0

For more Miss Anna books to love,
visit us at

w w w . m i s s a n n a b o o k s . c o m

Numbers are working hard all over the world!
Come Travel the World with Us!

www.ingramcontent.com/pod-product-compliance
Lightning Source LLC
Chambersburg PA
CBHW041100050726
47599CB00018B/2212